Soul Cleanse

2-in-1
Christian Adult Coloring Book & Journal

Grace Annan, LCSW, LICSW

This book is intended for educational and personal development purposes only. It is not a substitute for professional mental health, medical, or other professional advice.
If you are experiencing emotional distress or a mental health crisis, please seek help from a qualified professional or contact your local crisis line.

Printed in the United States of America

ISBN-13: 978-1732367623
ISBN-10: 1732367620

Living Life Learning
www.livinglifelearning.com

This book belongs to:

_____

Gifted by (optional):

_____

Date:

_____

Date _____

"Trust in the Lord with all your heart
and lean not on your own understanding;
in all your ways submit to Him,
and He will make your paths straight."
— Proverbs 3:5-6

Where in your life is God asking you to trust Him?

_____

_____

_____

_____

_____

_____

_____

_____

_____

_____

_____

_____

_____

_____

_____

_____

_____

_____

_____

_____

Trust Him

Date_____

*"I have set the LORD always before me;
because He is at my right hand,
I shall not be shaken."*
— Psalm 16:8

What helps you stay unshaken in hard times?

_____
_____
_____
_____
_____
_____
_____
_____
_____
_____
_____
_____
_____
_____
_____
_____
_____
_____
_____
_____
_____
_____

Grounded in God

Date_____

"May the God of hope fill you with all joy and peace
in believing, so that by the power of the Holy Spirit
you may abound in hope."
— Romans 15:13

Where do you need more peace and hope today?

_____

_____

_____

_____

_____

_____

_____

_____

_____

_____

_____

_____

_____

_____

_____

_____

_____

_____

_____

_____

_____

_____

Hope Flows

Date _____

"Casting all your anxieties on Him,
because He cares for you."
— 1 Peter 5:7

What do you need to release to God today?

_____

_____

_____

_____

_____

_____

_____

_____

_____

_____

_____

_____

_____

_____

_____

_____

_____

_____

_____

_____

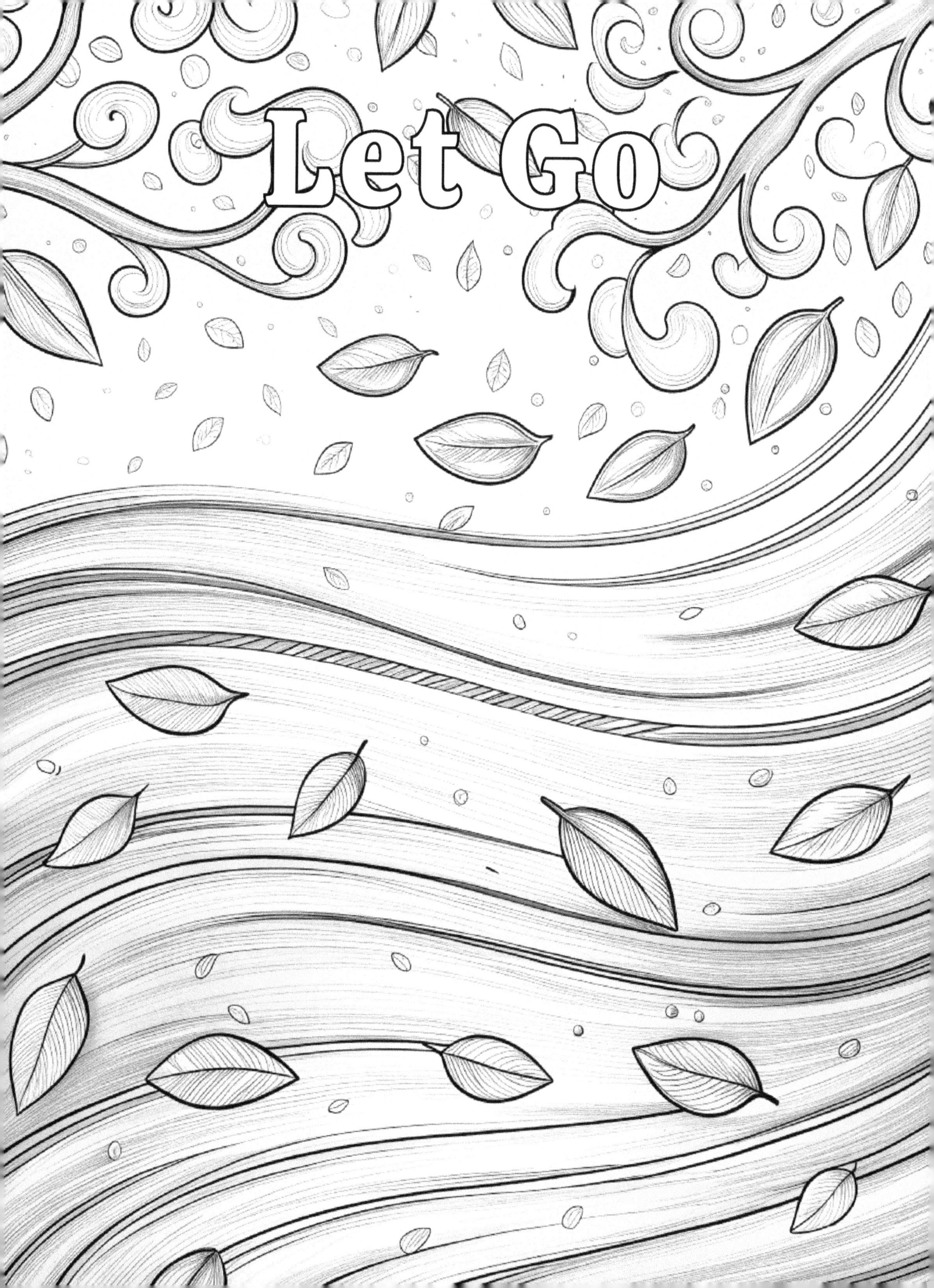

Let Go

Date _____

"The LORD is my light and my salvation;
whom shall I fear?
The LORD is the stronghold of my life;
of whom shall I be afraid?"
— Psalm 27:1

Where do you need God's light to overcome fear?

_____
_____
_____
_____
_____
_____
_____
_____
_____
_____
_____
_____
_____
_____
_____
_____
_____
_____
_____
_____
_____

Courage in Him

Date_____

*"For I know the plans I have for you, declares the
LORD, plans for welfare and not for evil,
to give you a future and a hope."*
— Jeremiah 29:11

What gives you hope for the future?

_____
_____
_____
_____
_____
_____
_____
_____
_____
_____
_____
_____
_____
_____
_____
_____
_____
_____
_____
_____
_____
_____

Date_____

"Peace I leave with you; My peace I give to you.
Not as the world gives do I give to you.
Let not your hearts be troubled,
neither let them be afraid."
— John 14:27

Where do you need Jesus' peace to calm your heart today?

_____
_____
_____
_____
_____
_____
_____
_____
_____
_____
_____
_____
_____
_____
_____
_____
_____
_____
_____
_____

Peace Within

Date _____

"Be still, and know that I am God."
— Psalm 46:10

What helps you be still in God's presence?

_____
_____
_____
_____
_____
_____
_____
_____
_____
_____
_____
_____
_____
_____
_____
_____
_____
_____
_____
_____

Be Still

Date_____

"This is the day that the LORD has made;
let us rejoice and be glad in it."
— Psalm 118:24

What are you grateful for today?

_____
_____
_____
_____
_____
_____
_____
_____
_____
_____
_____
_____
_____
_____
_____
_____
_____
_____
_____
_____
_____

Rejoice

Date _____

"But they who wait for the LORD shall renew their strength; they shall mount up with wings like eagles; they shall run and not be weary; they shall walk and not faint."
— Isaiah 40:31

Where do you need God's strength to carry you today?

_____
_____
_____
_____
_____
_____
_____
_____
_____
_____
_____
_____
_____
_____
_____
_____
_____
_____
_____
_____
_____

Renewed Strength

Date _____

"Love is patient and kind; love does not envy or boast; it is not arrogant or rude. It does not insist on its own way; it is not irritable or resentful; it does not rejoice at wrongdoing, but rejoices with the truth. Love bears all things, believes all things, hopes all things, endures all things."
— 1 Corinthians 13:4–7

Where can you show more patience or kindness today?

_____
_____
_____
_____
_____
_____
_____
_____
_____
_____
_____
_____
_____
_____
_____
_____
_____
_____
_____
_____

Love Always

Date_____

"Count it all joy, my brothers, when you meet trials
of various kinds, for you know that the testing of
your faith produces steadfastness."
— James 1:2–3

How can you find joy in what's challenging you right now?

_____
_____
_____
_____
_____
_____
_____
_____
_____
_____
_____
_____
_____
_____
_____
_____
_____
_____
_____
_____
_____

Date_____

"Commit your way to the LORD;
trust in Him, and He will act."
— Psalm 37:5

What would you like to place fully in God's hands?

_____

_____

_____

_____

_____

_____

_____

_____

_____

_____

_____

_____

_____

_____

_____

_____

_____

_____

_____

_____

_____

_____

_____

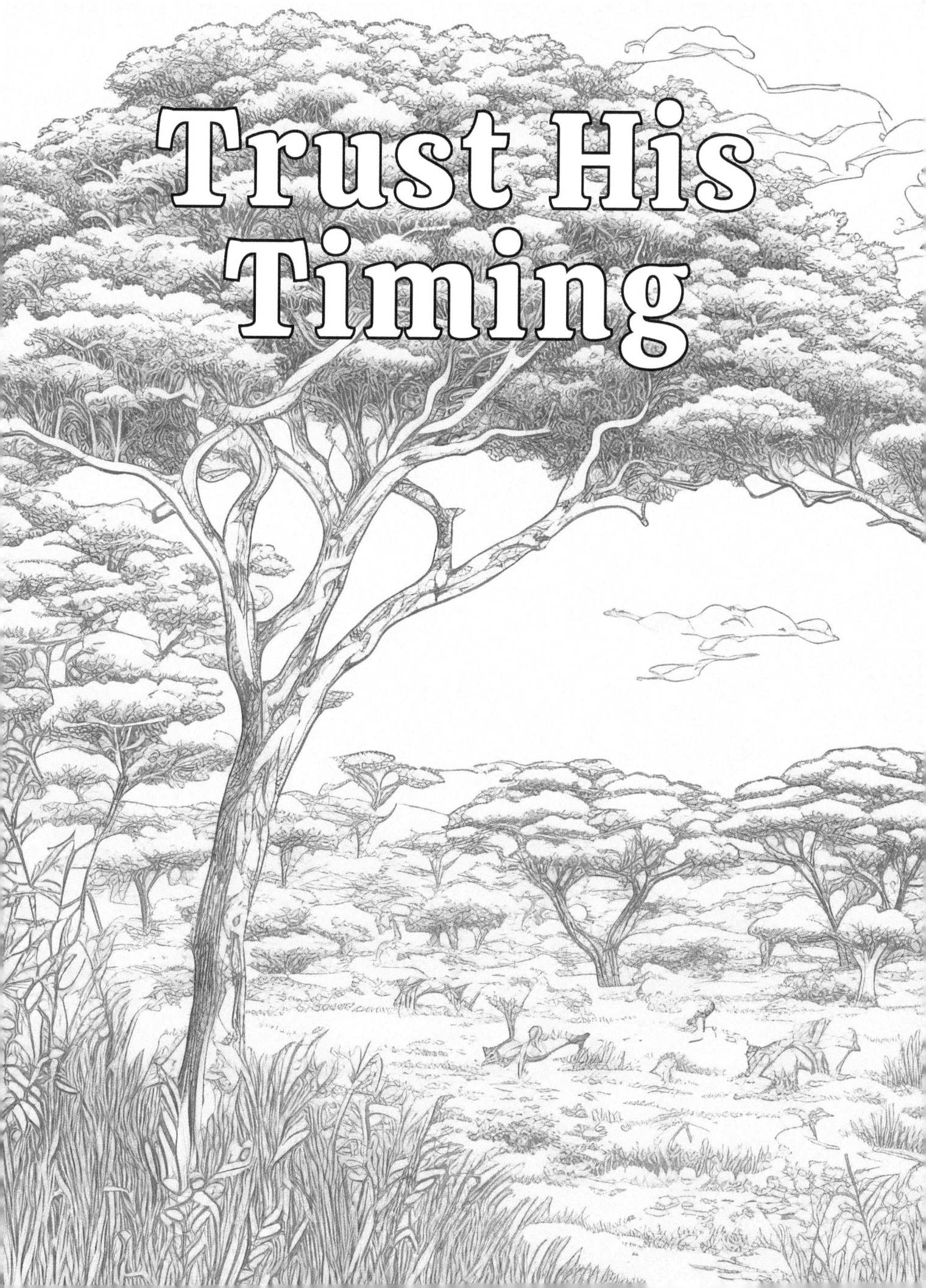

Trust His
Timing

Date _____

"Have I not commanded you? Be strong and courageous. Do not be frightened, and do not be dismayed, for the LORD your God is with you wherever you go."
— Joshua 1:9

Where do you need God's courage today?

_____
_____
_____
_____
_____
_____
_____
_____
_____
_____
_____
_____
_____
_____
_____
_____
_____
_____
_____
_____
_____

Courage in Faith

Date_____

"And my God will supply every need of yours
according to His riches in glory in Christ Jesus."
— Philippians 4:19

Where have you seen God provide for you recently?

_____
_____
_____
_____
_____
_____
_____
_____
_____
_____
_____
_____
_____
_____
_____
_____
_____
_____
_____
_____
_____
_____
_____
_____

God Provides

Date _____

"Bless the LORD, O my soul,
and forget not all His benefits."
— Psalm 103:2

What blessings come to mind as you reflect today?

_____

_____

_____

_____

_____

_____

_____

_____

_____

_____

_____

_____

_____

_____

_____

_____

_____

_____

_____

_____

_____

Give Thanks

Date _____

"The steadfast love of the LORD never ceases;
His mercies never come to an end;
they are new every morning;
great is Your faithfulness."
— Lamentations 3:22–23

How has God shown you His faithfulness recently?

_____

_____

_____

_____

_____

_____

_____

_____

_____

_____

_____

_____

_____

_____

_____

_____

_____

_____

_____

_____

_____

_____

New Mercies

Date_____

"Create in me a clean heart, O God,
and renew a right spirit within me."
— *Psalm 51:10*

What would you like God to renew within you?

_____
_____
_____
_____
_____
_____
_____
_____
_____
_____
_____
_____
_____
_____
_____
_____
_____
_____
_____
_____
_____
_____

Clean Heart

Date _____

"You have turned for me my mourning into
dancing; You have loosed my sackcloth
and clothed me with gladness."
— Psalm 30:11

Where has God brought joy out of pain in your life?

_____

_____

_____

_____

_____

_____

_____

_____

_____

_____

_____

_____

_____

_____

_____

_____

_____

_____

_____

_____

Clothed in Gladness

Date_____

"And the peace of God, which surpasses all understanding, will guard your hearts and your minds in Christ Jesus."
— Philippians 4:7

What does God's peace feel like to you today?

_____
_____
_____
_____
_____
_____
_____
_____
_____
_____
_____
_____
_____
_____
_____
_____
_____
_____
_____
_____
_____
_____

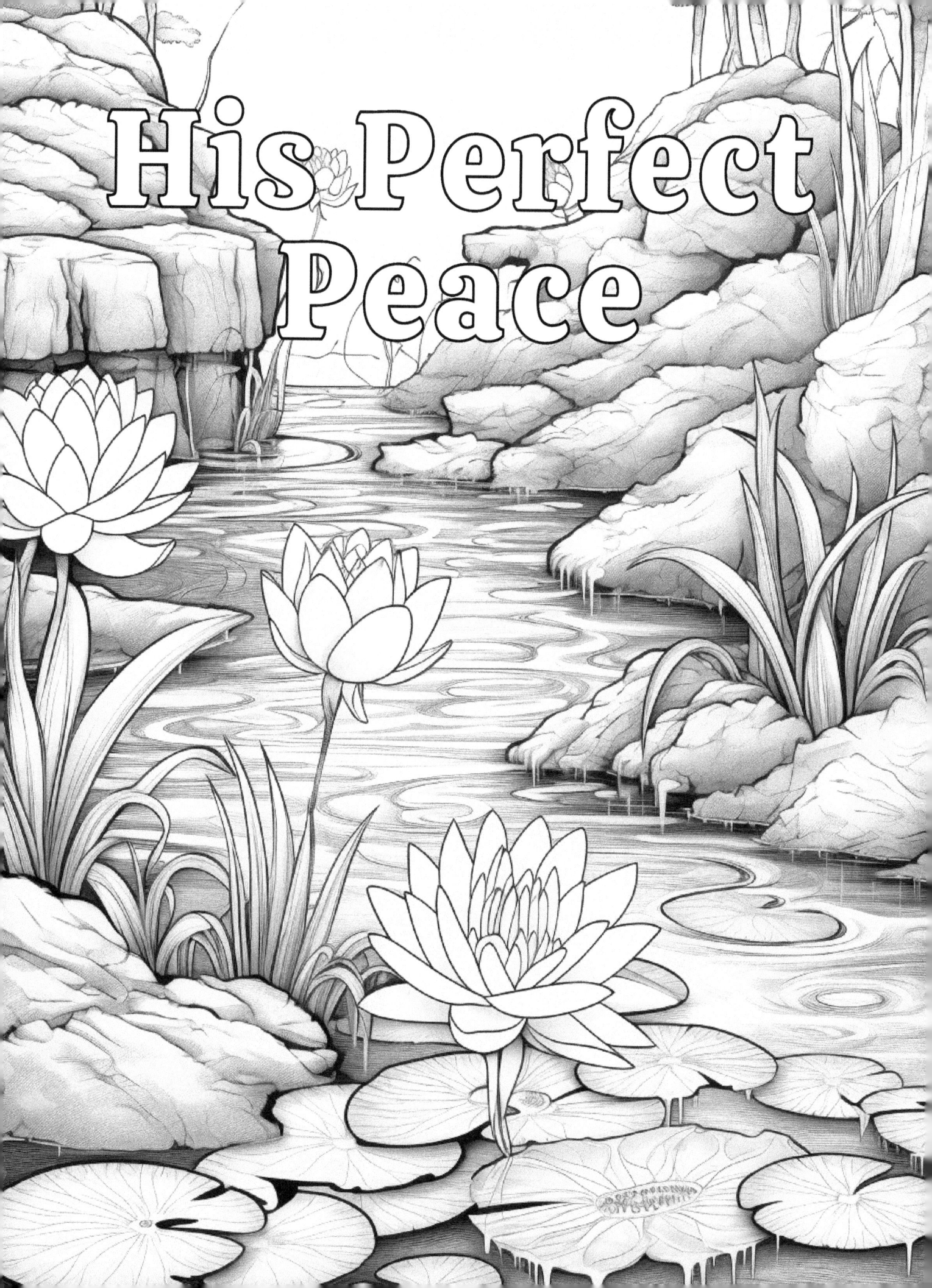

His Perfect
Peace

Date_____

"For the LORD is good;
His steadfast love endures forever,
and His faithfulness to all generations."
— Psalm 100:5

How has God's goodness shown up in your life this week?

_____

_____

_____

_____

_____

_____

_____

_____

_____

_____

_____

_____

_____

_____

_____

_____

_____

_____

_____

_____

_____

_____

God Is Good

Date _____

"The heart of man plans his way,
but the LORD establishes his steps."
— Proverbs 16:9

Where have you seen God directing your steps unexpectedly?

_____

_____

_____

_____

_____

_____

_____

_____

_____

_____

_____

_____

_____

_____

_____

_____

_____

_____

_____

_____

_____

Guided by Grace

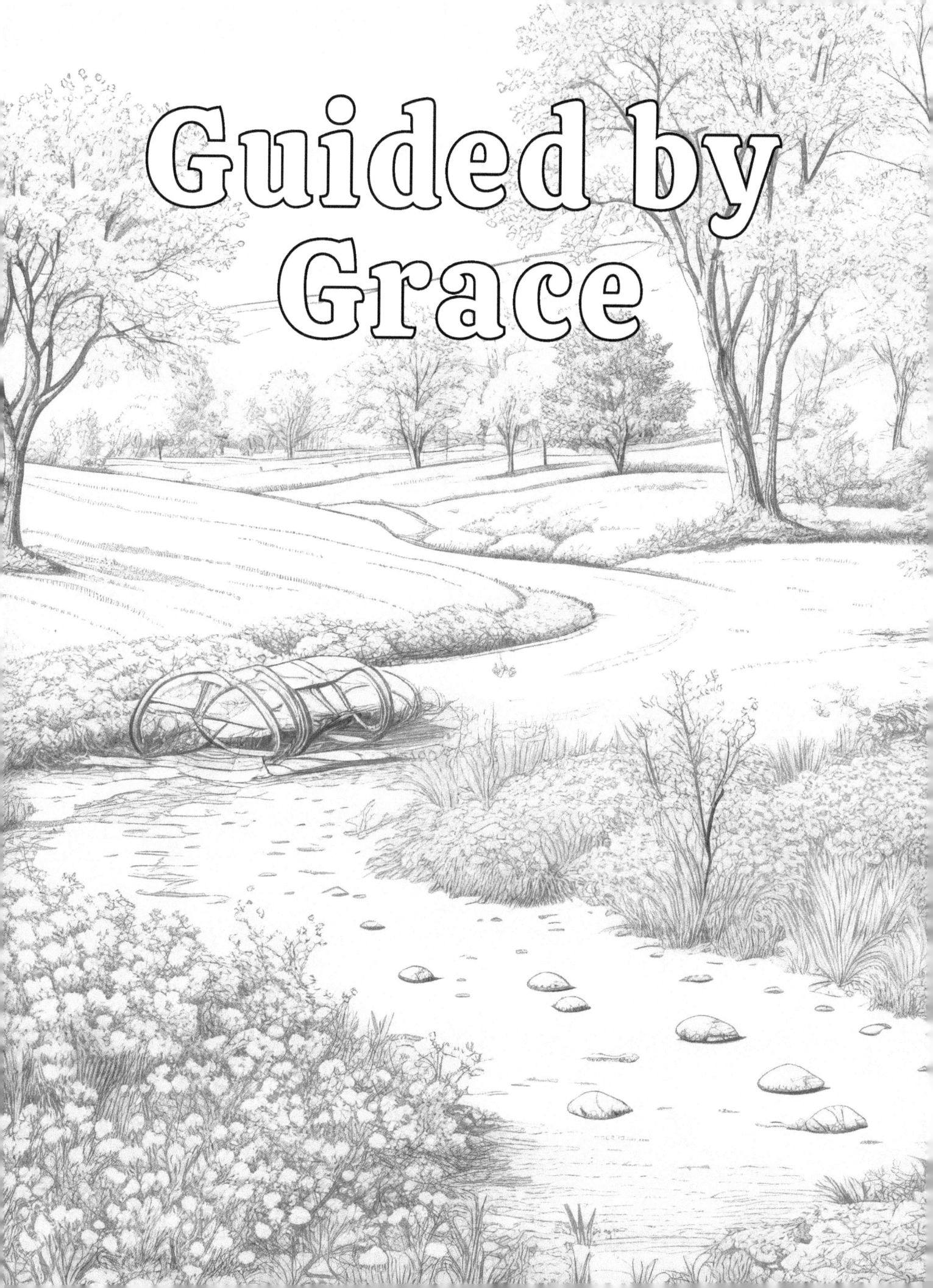

Date _____

"Fear not, for I am with you;
be not dismayed, for I am your God;
I will strengthen you, I will help you,
I will uphold you with my righteous right hand."
— Isaiah 41:10

What helps you remember He's with you?

_____

_____

_____

_____

_____

_____

_____

_____

_____

_____

_____

_____

_____

_____

_____

_____

_____

_____

_____

_____

_____

_____

Held by His Hand

Date_____

"Delight yourself in the LORD,
and He will give you the desires of your heart."
— Psalm 37:4

What does delighting in God look like for you right now?

_____

_____

_____

_____

_____

_____

_____

_____

_____

_____

_____

_____

_____

_____

_____

_____

_____

_____

_____

_____

Delight in Him

Date_____

*"I will instruct you and teach you in the way you
should go; I will counsel you with My eye upon you."*
— *Psalm 32:8*

Where do you sense God guiding you right now?

_____

_____

_____

_____

_____

_____

_____

_____

_____

_____

_____

_____

_____

_____

_____

_____

_____

_____

_____

_____

_____

_____

_____

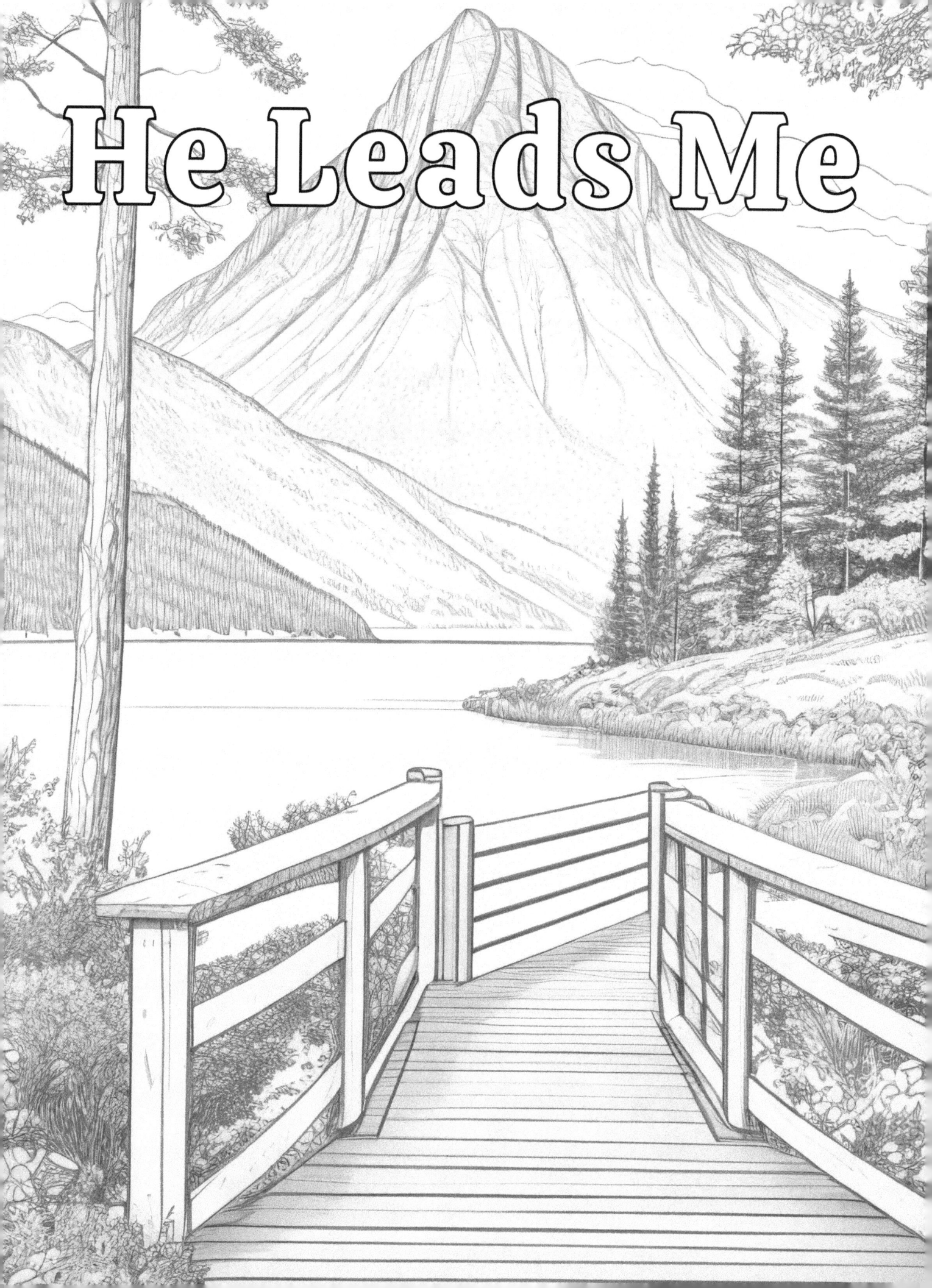

He Leads Me

Date_____

*"My flesh and my heart may fail,
but God is the strength of my heart and my portion forever."*
— Psalm 73:26

What helps you remember God is your strength?

_____
_____
_____
_____
_____
_____
_____
_____
_____
_____
_____
_____
_____
_____
_____
_____
_____
_____
_____
_____
_____
_____

My Strength Forever

Date _____

"Rejoice in hope, be patient in tribulation,
be constant in prayer."
— Romans 12:12

How can you stay hopeful in hard times?

_____
_____
_____
_____
_____
_____
_____
_____
_____
_____
_____
_____
_____
_____
_____
_____
_____
_____
_____
_____
_____

Joy in Hope

Date_____

"Peace I leave with you; My peace I give to you.
Not as the world gives do I give to you.
Let not your hearts be troubled, neither let them be afraid."
— John 14:27

What helps you rest in God's peace today?

_____
_____
_____
_____
_____
_____
_____
_____
_____
_____
_____
_____
_____
_____
_____
_____
_____
_____
_____
_____

Perfect Peace

Date_____

"But He said to me, 'My grace is sufficient for you,
for My power is made perfect in weakness.'"
— 2 Corinthians 12:9

How can you lean on God's grace right now?

_____
_____
_____
_____
_____
_____
_____
_____
_____
_____
_____
_____
_____
_____
_____
_____
_____
_____
_____
_____
_____
_____

Sufficient Grace

Date _____

"Let the words of my mouth and the meditation of my heart
be acceptable in Your sight,
O LORD, my rock and my redeemer."
— Psalm 19:14

What thoughts or words do you want to offer to God today?

_____

_____

_____

_____

_____

_____

_____

_____

_____

_____

_____

_____

_____

_____

_____

_____

_____

_____

_____

_____

_____

My Rock and Redeemer

About the Author

Grace Annan, LCSW, LICSW, is a licensed therapist, author, and creator with a heart for helping others find peace, clarity, and spiritual renewal. Through her work, she combines her background in mental and emotional wellness with her Christian faith to create resources that heal the mind and uplift the spirit. She is also the founder of Living Life Learning and Wholemindedly (on Amazon), where she designs tools that inspire reflection, growth, and inner calm.

Explore More

If you enjoyed Soul Cleanse, continue your journey of peace and renewal with Grace's other reflective works designed to support emotional healing and spiritual growth.

The Guided Reset Series (Volumes 1–3)
A 90-day, 3-volume 2-in-1 guided journal and coloring book series created to help you build calm, resilience, and renewal. Each volume offers four weeks of daily reflections, mindfulness and somatic practices, and therapeutic journaling prompts crafted to gently strengthen your inner peace one day at a time.

Whether you are nurturing your faith, restoring your calm, or rediscovering yourself after a challenging season, The Guided Reset invites you to slow down, breathe, and reconnect with peace, one page at a time.

www.ingramcontent.com/pod-product-compliance
Lightning Source LLC
Chambersburg PA
CBHW081250040426
42452CB00015B/2771